Randomness

Poetry

By

D. B. Barker

ISBN: 978-1720752622
ISBN-13: 1720752621

DEDICATION

To my muse, my soul mate, my wife,
Debbi Barker

CONTENTS

RANDOMNESS

1 MEMORIES

As I walk alone in body,
in mind and spirit,
I walk with thee
which makes me full of glee.
Oh, how I won't let go through my memories.
I still hold you near, my dear.
I know you're looking back at me
as you wait for me,
to always be side by side
still walking and talking oblivious to all.
I'm often sitting alone with a tear in my eye.
Sometimes I even cry.
Oh, how I wish I had longer with you,
taken way too soon.
Oh, how I still miss you.
If only you could come back just for a few days,
a few hours,
a few minutes
so we could chat and walk like we used to do.
It's not the same alone these days,
as my memories start to fade,
but I still walk everyday thinking of you.
As looks fade with age, it almost fills me with rage.
So what if I'm showing some signs of my age?
I'm no disgrace,
still a person.
Don't be embarrassed by me.

Take me out,
or I will have no memories of thee, and family,
to take with me.
Forget old conflicts.
It's time to let it go,
to return to being a family.
Memories are like whispers from your past
drawing you in,
mere shadows of what has been
or what could have been

2 AGE

As for a mirror, we won't bother with that.
With age comes less grace
but still I'm no disgrace for my age.
Some say I'm ugly,
all wrinkly.
Well, I don't mean to be;
it's what life has given me.
So
it's do I die now and avoid my fate by creating my
own?
Or: do I have enough to keep on going?
There is still life in this old man's bones.
I don't need a retirement home
just yet.
At night I watch the moon go down,
and the night fade fast into the next day.
I lay alone,
looking at my dentures floating in their glass,
wishing I had someone to fetch me a tea that's not
a carer,
and me to get tea for them.
To just cuddle up once more is all I ask,
skin on skin.
The warmth of a human,
not my hot water bottle.
Age has its regrets like getting tattoos on my chest
that now hang on my belly.

From my bicep to my elbow
it looked good once.
I was told growing old
with someone next to you
is a pleasure indeed.
Maybe there is time to find a new soulmate.
Simple things in life work best.
Remember you're never too old
to hold hands.
Age means nothing to me really.
I still hear the words: "What's he up to now?"
as I do things to keep myself young.
I'm not that old,
just in body not in my youthful mind.
I hope people remember me
for the good times,
not the sad times.

3 LIFE

Life is an opportunity given to you.
Don't abuse it,
live it.
Enjoy it while you can.
Life sometimes goes wrong as I sit alone,
all alone in my home.
I think my guardian angel is broken,
no better than my garden gnome
really.
As life goes by and these wrongs come along,
don't dwell, move along.
Get a taste for it
and live it all the way.
Just don't gamble with it.
Sometimes life lets you leave
a past behind
to find a new you and a better life
with no regrets.
Take each step a day at a time.
Life lets you be who you want to be
(if you do it right).
Sometimes gentle,
sometimes so strong.
Sometimes life goes wrong.
Life sails by.
Life is a trip with a start and an end,
a new one in, an old one out.

That's what life is all about.
As in a book, turn the page
life goes on that way.

4 DREAMS

Dreams come in all sizes, some large, some small.
You can't remember them all.
Dreams can come true, it's often up to you.
They can last a lifetime
if you want them to.
Remember them, hold on to them,
don't let them fade.
Dreams feel so real as you play out what you're
dreaming about.
Sometimes you awaken
a little shaken
with a dream memory, good or bad.
To find the dream from once before can't be done.
You close your eyes and try,
but that dream has passed you by.
A daydream is often wishful thinking.
Sitting or standing or traveling by car or train,
you daydream away.
Sitting on a park bench,
watching the clouds float on by.
Passing the time the right way.
Dreams are what keep you going.
So, dream away,
bcause when dreams stop,
life stops.
Lights fading away,
goodbye,
no more dreams for me.

5 HOPES AND WISHES

Hope is having the knowledge that life is full of
opportunities and that miracles can and will
happen.
Hope is knowing that changes can happen for the
better.
Hope brings you strength to know it will get better.
Believe in it.
Don't lose hope;
things happen.
People will be around,
and then no more,
but don't let it shut a door.
With hope there will always be
other doors for you to explore.
Wouldn't you just like to wish away all the woes in
the world?
Money troubles or health troubles, you wish them
all away
then wish some more.
A dream maybe?
Wish it anyway,
it could come true someday.
Birthday wishes.
Christmas wishes.
Secret wishes.
Shooting star far away,
just wish away.
Believe in it,

and watch your wishes come true.
Just don't wish your life away,
it will happen someday.
Don't wish for it too soon,
hopes and wishes.

6 MONEY

So, you're lucky enough to always be on the go,
spending money
like it's found on the ground.
From more shoes than you can wear,
to too many jewels,
you have brought it all.
Really, you're not upper-class,
you're just a back-street lass.
You can't buy real friends,
on that you can depend.
Arrogant as hell,
when you leave a room
a foul smell leaves too:
the smell of "look how much money I've got".
It sounds like you're lonely, and friendship poor.
Left only with money by your side.
You're counting your money,
and still wanting more.
The type of person who would empty a wishing-
well,
not giving a damn about the poor,
just to have more
than anyone else.
Alone in your great big home,
waiting for money trees to grow.
Greed comes to mind,
a breed not loved by everyone.
Your money doesn't make you
better than me

7 FAMILY

Family are there to share.
Be it your sorrow, or a burden,
or happier times.
Time to share with a family that care,
to take the evil away
and bring in the good.
Family will always come together,
maybe by a fine tether
but truly never far away.
For sickness or health,
often standing side by side,
they find a way to make it better
with their strength and love.
As the links clink
on your family chain,
family care for you
and about you.
You've never been truly alone
when you have family keeping home,
no matter how far you roam.
A special family
who will always remember thee,
don't let them drift away.
Stay in touch,
let them know how you are.
Let them know where you are,
to ready a welcome when you return home.
Share time with your family,

as it's not the same when they are gone.
A void that can't be filled:
family.

8 MY PLACE

My place is walking through the trees, taking in
nature's breeze,
listening and feeling nature passing by.
The sun high in the sky,
as birds fly silently by.

Or is my place at the beach,
taking in the sun and pleasure
from everyone?
I like to watch the waves break
and see the adults and children run
when they get too close to the sea,
just for the fun of it.
Enjoying the sun whilst eating ice-cream.
The seafront seems so peaceful,
even though it's full of
hustle and bustle.
Everyone in their own little place of happiness,
as time slips idly by.
It could be in a hotel room,
leaning on a balcony,
food and drinks thrown in.
Or a sporty car,
a drive in the country,
a picnic just for you and me
and a scenic slow drive back to the hotel.
Loving the swimming pool,
just me and you.

Others are there but we do not see.
Or is it home?
Next to you:
that's my place
I reckon.

9 HATE

Hate will consume you
from the outside right through
to the inside.
Hate can fill you with rage;
you need to turn the page
and write the next chapter.
Let hate disintegrate.
Hate will grate against its natural enemy of love.
Don't love to hate,
just love.
It's better, anyway.
Hate.
Making me sick on the inside.
Showing on the outside.
Hate doesn't help you look great.
Hate stands for you.
You're so fake.
I would hurt you for all the hate that's in me,
but you're not worth it.
I'm not giving you the satisfaction
of seeing me fall apart.
So, you can blame me.
I so hate you right now,
but I'm better than you.
Go on, hate me back.
I'm satisfied to watch the hate
eat away at you,
as my hate disintegrates.

10 PERFECT PARTNER

My perfect partner can be miles away,
even islands away,
and I close my eyes and there you are.
I end up falling for you all the more.
My perfect partner.
Each day I wake up with you,
my butterflies don't go away, they just flutter
more,
leaving me to love you all the more.
The one thing I did right in life
was finding you and
passing you my heart.
My perfect partner holds my heart.
I know she won't drop or hurt it.
She cuddles up to it as I do to hers.
It makes me complete.
It makes us complete.
We're both imperfect and that's
what makes it perfect,
a lifetime love affair.
Seeing you cry makes me cry,
I don't know why.
So, let's not see a tear in that eye,
keep it dry
because I love you, my perfect partner.

11 LOVE

Love me and I'll always be
by your side,
your friend in whom to confide,
your guide and lover beside.
Love taught me you are the one,
my lover who I fell for from the start,
my forever sweetheart.
We're so in tune.
You bring laughter when tears are near.
It was easy to fall deeply in love with you,
with the things you do and
the things you don't do,
never too demanding.
I love it all
and more.
And I thought the love in me had died,
after a rough ride,
until you came by my side.
And in fact, love was only
off to one side.
Now it's back,
and you make me intact
once more.
My heart is cold no more.
It burns with fire once more.
Seasons merge
as you bloom every day
in the most romantic way.
I love you.

12 DARKNESS

Darkness
is where I feel at home.
Walking on the edge,
looking outward at thee.
Darkness does encompass me;
walking in its shadows feeling hollow.
I embrace it as it comforts me,
just one step in and I disappear
until I want to reappear.
My heart is nothing but darkness
full of shadows and blackness,
hurt and hate.
Black is all I want to score,
I can't fight it anymore.
Darkness will be my forever home.
In the darkness I'm confident and strong,
it's truly where I belong.
A nightmare is where you will see me next
as you lay unable to scream.
I bring demons with me.
You do right to fear me
from in the light.
From the darkness I will come.
You will be mine.
If you are in a tunnel with me,
no light at the end will you see.
I am a nightmare within you,
be warned.

Have a nice dream tonight
and I might come by
to give you a fright.
From the darkness I see light.
I see you.

13 WEATHER

A drop of rain
rolls down the window pane
as the weather changes again.
Dark clouds bring the rain again,
but it's not all bad.
With rain comes new life
through the liquid water.
Rain clouds move noisily along,
bringing along a sunny spell.
That would be swell.
The rougher weather is no more than mother
nature in a mood,
throwing a tantrum,
throwing her weight around.
As the wind comes in the clouds
darken
and lightening briefly brightens,
bringing heavy rains.
Then the weather
throws in some snow,
then it lightens,
and bright sun again.
So hot that people moan,
that's our crazy weather
with no pattern.
Winter brings the deepest chill,
with more than waft of snow
which is no thrill,

leaving many hating their winter chill.
It has to get worse to get better,
so take a pill
to get rid of that chill.
The weather is changing again.

14 DANCE

Close your eyes
and let the music wake you.
Let it put a smile on your face,
and dance your worries away.
Don't dance with the pack to fit in
be different and do your own thing.
Wiggle that bum,
whirl and twirl
as if no one is looking.
Be yourself, and dance.
If you can't dance, do a dad dance.
Just dance for you.
With shoes, without shoes,
it's up to you.
You have to
dance outside.
Alone or with someone,
an open sky up above,
a perfect clear night sky
with stars lighting your dance floor.
Go on, give it some more.
You'll be happy for ever more.
All eyes on you as you take to the floor,
think no more.
Just let the rhythm take you.
Dance as if no audience is there,
and no one can say

you can't dance.
At least you're up there
enjoying yourself.
That's what dancing is all about.

15 WINNING

Winning can keep you grinning,
but always be gracious in defeat.
Don't throw a tantrum
or act childish,
and don't weep.
You're better than that.
Not winning is no disgrace.
It's just the beginning,
soon enough you will be winning, and grinning.
Don't watch the others with one eye.
Focus your eye on
where you're going,
and simply keep going.
Just try.
Fight to be a winner.
Work for it during the day,
and all night if need be.
Train for it.
Desire it.
Winning is it.
Just taking part is winning it.
Crossing that line
at any time
is winning it.
If you keep on loving, you're winning.
Keep on earning, you're winning.
Keep on living, you're winning.

16 JEALOUSY

Jealousy takes you,
grips you.
not letting go,
pulling you to and fro.
Jealousy fills you with
fear and anger,
maybe inadequacy,
certainly anxiety,
and insecurity.
Jealousy torments you every second of every day.
Hide it well and maybe
no one can tell,
but you feel
poison flooding through.
It's an emotion that is harder
to switch off,
than it is to switch on.
It always leaves a bitter aftertaste.
Often heartbroken,
I never want to lose you.
Love me, not another.
Jealousy is from light grey,
to the blackest black.
That's where jealousy is at with me.
From the darkest corners of my mind,
jealousy hits me when I thought
I had hidden it well,
controlled it.
No, jealousy controls me.

17 SWEARING

Swearing is so wearing and unbecoming of you,
yet swearing is all you do.
Do you think swearing makes you bigger,
or even better, than all around you?
Swearing is costing you at family times.
With friends and neighbours
it all wears thin,
and gets under people's skin,
often offending all those about you.
Swearing in a moment of
anger or pain is fine.
It goes away in a short time.
But to do it all the time
makes you weak,
maybe you should shut your beak.
Use a swear jar,
don't swear about the swear jar,
it will cost you money
not friends and family.
Learn to express yourself without the need of
swearing.
As you get older,
your swearing is getting more frequent,
not less.
A senior up to no good,
using words of anger and hatred,
full of spite.
It ain't right.

Swearing and belching
and farting your way home,
alone.

18 REFLECTION

My reflection in the mirror is of me that I see.
Or is it what I want or wish
to see staring back at me?
A likeness that's stronger than me,
not the real weak me looking back.
My reflection is staring at me,
haunting me, punishing me.
Just an empty likeness of me,
of what could have been I suppose.
Is it he?
Or me?
Hidden away during the day,
only leaving my home alone at night
so no one can see the real me.
That reflection of me is why I
can't see thee.
I'm just too ugly.
No longer youthful, just woeful.
It can't be undone.
Too many flaws for all too see,
and that's just the reflection looking back at me.
What must you think of me?
I have a heart
that you or I can't see,
but it's as scarred as the rest of me,
a poor reflection of me.
I'm sorry.
Enjoy your life without me holding you back.

Don't look back at me.
My reflection already has to do that,
you've no need.

19 PARTY

Time to party.
Get dressed up all smarty,
to head to the party.
With music and food in abundance
I do a little happy dance.
I love to party,
be it a tea party,
or a firemen's leaving party.
I am a true party animal.
All the attention is on me,
as I'm the life of any party.
There is no party without me.
Go on! Come along for some fun,
don't be the boring one.
There will be no morning after,
it will just carry on.
Let's party!
Halloween party can't be beaten
with everyone in fancy-dress
from their head to their feet.
I can't stress enough:
party on.
I'm tapping my feet
to an invisible beat
when there is no party.

20 TALES AROUND THE CAMPFIRE

Tales.
Some are fine,
some are of the dark kind.
Bear in mind,
some are of the
very frightening kind.
Not fairy tales;
no happy endings here.
The open fire and the darkness makes the tree line
seem closer.
As it flickers away you see shadows darting around.
You hear a sound.
You are sure you see something looking back at
you.
You are sure it's eyeshine,
reflecting the fire's glittering light.
Is it there, or is it not there?
Throwing more wood on the fire lets off sparks
and your brain does the same
as you start to imagine
the tales are real,
and about to happen to you
as you sit there
and just stare
at the fire's embers
as if they weren't there,
wishing you weren't there.
After hearing the campfire stories

there comes sleeping in the tent.
With shadows creeping in,
there goes that noise again.
Something's out there.
Does no one care?
Will I ever sleep again?
I'm really wishing I hadn't come along.
Camping may not be for me.
Daylight, not moonlight, for me.

21 EYES

Looking at your eyes
will tell me what's on your mind and
I react.
Looking at your eyes, they don't lie.
They return my love for you.
We don't need to speak,
our eyes do the talking.
When I close my eyes
I still see you standing there
with your hair so fair.
My eyes don't cry
when you are there,
only when you're not there.
You have those come-to-bed eyes,
or this-is-for-life eyes.
Well, I wish for them both.
Eyes speak without speaking,
all about you,
and yet tell it all.
You can paint your face and
colour your lips,
and brush on eyeshadow,
but those eyes don't lie to me.
They tell all —
you're in love with me.
Eyes often tell a story,
and for me it's a love story.
I found those eyes and dived right in,
and now I wake up to those eyes every morning.

22 SAYING GOODBYE

Goodbye is more than just a
sad word.
It finalises something.
An angel finding her wings once more
and returning home.
I'm sure as I watched you fade,
I heard the wings flutter by.
How many times have we said goodbye?
This time was the final goodbye.
It made me cry.
We said goodbye
but I won't lie,
it hurt me,
knowing we would never say
good morning again.
But I still have you in my dreams
my memories over time may fade
but they won't dissipate.
There every time I dream of you,
too short a time I had with you.
I wanted to spend my entire life
with you.
I have no regrets for all the time spent with you,
good and bad, happy and sad.
I will remember my love for you
I will tend the earth above you,
until I join you,
goodbye.

23 GOSSIP

You can get all the latest
from someone
who had promised to keep
what they said a secret.
That's a gossip.
A good rule you should follow
is
'don't repeat what you have been told'
especially through a third party.
Simply put,
if you were not there,
if you didn't see it with your own eyes,
or hear it with your own ears,
don't repeat it.
That's idle gossip.
It's saddening how some people have become so
jealous of someone else, and possibly insecure,
that they say things,
really nasty things,
without knowing the person personally.
making it up as they go along.
Don't try to gossip,
unless you have trodden their footsteps before.
If you want to know more,
ask the person concerned.
It can start too easily:
just tell a friend.
That friend tells a friend,
and the gossip is well underway.
This is not swell

after a promise not to tell.
Think to yourself,
- is it going to cause harm?
- is it even true?
- could it harm you?
Yes, maybe, you don't know.
So, don't gossip, leave it alone.
It has nothing to do with you.

24 EVALUATE

There will be many times in a life when you need to
stop and evaluate
what you are and where you are going.
Take stepping stones along the way
so as not to get your feet wet.
Address whatever comes along to get your life back
on song.
Evaluate any damage caused to you.
Can you escape?
Don't make the same mistake twice.
When it's all going wrong,
pause and think.
Not after it's gone wrong.
That's too late.
Not another mistake
is the time to evaluate.
Stop! before it is too late.
Evaluate, and levitate yourself
out of any situation.
Retaliate, if it helps you out.
Evaluate every decision.
There's no delete or rewind with real life.
Not if you want to carry on living.

25 THINK

Windows are made to ponder through.
Let your imagination wander through.
Going out and about,
lots to think about.
Like, what holds up a cloud?
Or what's up there
looking down
at me looking back up at it
not even knowing it?
I like to think of you
when I'm not with you.
I think of you all the time,
with a smile so proud on my face,
just like when I'm walking beside you.
I'm not sure it's healthy to always think about you,
but I am obsessed with you.
I think of all the things we have done:
watched a rainbow rise then fade away,
stood outside on a rainy day,
seen a birth,
seen a death,
spent time at a grave,
spent personal time, just you and me,
sitting under our favourite tree.
I think I'm the happiest man alive
to have you by my side.
Do you ever think like that of me?

26 SORRY

Sorry is such a hard word to say when you've been
wrong
or done wrong.
Knowing you're wrong can be just as hard.
But actually,
saying sorry helps a lot
to make amends for
what's been done.
I've let you down once again.
It may only be a starting point,
but it is a start,
and should be the full stop.
I know, believe me,
that I'm not perfect,
truly far from perfect,
but I'm me.
Sorry. Please forgive me.
Sorry for the pain.
I'm in denial no more,
it was me.
Forgive me,
and stay by my side.
Sorry for the rough ride.
I do repent it.
I'm sorry for the tears you shed.
It should have been me
crying instead.
No more lies.

No more getting mad.
And I should talk more.
Sorry is such a small word,
and you deserve so much more
but it has to start somewhere.
Sorry.

27 MUSIC

Music lets you lose yourself
just as you doubt yourself.
Music lets you live again
if only in your mind.
Music is like life:
it has its high notes
as well as its low notes,
with some floating
like a chorus in between.
Dance to your own rhythm.
Maybe life's stalled
getting too repetitive.
You need to shuffle,
as you do your music collection,
to get to the songs you like.
Do the same to get
the life you would like.
Music's beat is like a heartbeat,
as you float helplessly
down the river of life.
Music is the sound of life.
Let the beat continue into old age.
With music, taste is so varied.
Let the rhythm take hold,
it will go on until your last heartbeat,
then they will play your favourite music beat and
they will never forget you.
Music gives so much.

Heartbeat and music beat
were in time,
always in tune,
then no more.

28 WATCHING

I lay watching you every night,
following your every breath.
Watching your chest rise and fall,
with every sexy breath you take.
I don't need sleep when I'm next to you,
I just want to watch you.
Going to work, being away from you, hurts me
through and through,
like anywhere that I can't watch you.
Every work day I'm in a hurry to get home so I can
watch you
some more.
I don't even notice if the TV's on,
as long as I'm next to you.
As I watch over you,
oh, how I love you.
Daytime watching is coming for me,
as I set up mini cameras
just to watch thee
when I'm at work on my phone.
It will all be fine.
I will tell you sometime.
No need to worry,
I'm not obsessed with thee.
It's for security.
I worry about you,
and watching you helps me.

29 SMILE

A smile helps the day on its way.
Smile to start the day, every day.
Smile even if you're trying to reconcile.
A smile is worthwhile.
A smile will bring back a smile
ten-fold.
A smile infection is not a bad thing.
Go on, show those dimples.
Go on, let the smile attack.
Let your smile create a warmth on a cold winter's
afternoon.
Let others swoon at your infectious splendid smile,
a smile so intoxicating.
Just remember,
a smile is free
a gift from thee,
only enriching those that receive.
Smile when sad or mad.
Smile if your hurt or feel bad.
For those without a smile,
give them one of yours.
A gift worth giving,
smile all the while.

30 GUILT

Guilt - a word about a wrong doing,
betrayal or offense.
Worse, a violation.
Possibly a regret,
or guilt by association
The real question is, do you feel it?
Understand it, or hide it?
How long will it stay hidden,
before you are guilt ridden?
Some use it wrongly.
To suffer guilt, you have to feel it,
to take the responsibility for it.
Such a bad demon to hold inside,
let it outside,
and apologise.
Make amends,
whatever it takes to lessen
the burden of guilt,
or it will take you in the end.
Sneaking a cake or a bake
or a biscuit or three
is no reason to feel guilt,
it's just a treat for thee,
and thus
guilt free.

31 SOCIAL MEDIA

Social media:
the young don't know life without it,
or how we survived before it.
The old detest it.
They won't use it.
They would rather talk face to face,
something the young are losing the ability to do.
They only know screen time,
they use a telephone all the time,
for everything other than making a call.
They often stumble, then trip and fall.
They lay flat on the floor
taking a selfie
hurt or not.
Life is there for all to see
with little or no privacy
be it tablet
phone or pc.
Social media:
it does give a voice for all
but is that a good thing?
Social media will soon be in our heads, not outward
electronically,
but inwardly
built inside our heads.
No escape, as the future owns us.
Our eyes seeing all around the world.
Not just before them,

anything except what's in front of them.
Social media grows
as the human slows.
Going backwards
by trying to go forwards.

32 ALONE

The streets are full of vibe and life moving by
as I sit here alone.
Daytime and night-time
come and go.
People pass by my home.
I'm so alone.
Getting old has no advantage for me
as I get to be more alone.
I'm forgetting the use of speech.
Birthdays bring a card,
but it's the wrong name and address.
My only brief excitement
as I thought someone had remembered me,
quickly returning to being alone
in my empty
cold, stale, home.
Christmas comes,
and I eat my bread and butter,
maybe a small cake
to sort of celebrate.
No cards,
no presents
to be undone,
not a single one,
not even from me.
Soon, no doubt,
they will want to put me in a home.
I don't want to go in their home,

I'd rather be alone.
I want to die in my home,
familiar surroundings for so long.
Let me do that at least.
To die alone, in my home,
is my last wish.

33 DON'T QUIT

When it's tough and rough in life
don't quit.
To quit is to admit failure.
Carry on.
Commit, and accomplish
all before you.
No one admires a quitter.
Things often go wrong
as life moves along,
so what if you got it wrong?
Make amends, and you win in the end.
Go up that hill,
Don't walk up that hill -
run -
knowing you'll soon be going down the other side
of that hill.
Just don't quit before you reach the end.
Carry on,
and reap the rewards of not being a quitter,
just the benefits of being a winner.
Permit others to help
before you give in.
If you quit,
you quit on them too.
Stay strong.
If you quit doesn't mean you were wrong,
just that you've moved along.

34 TIME

It used to be tick-tock on a big old clock.
Now it's just a silent digital screen.
Time has moved on.
We all wish time would pause,
or at least slow down.
Life starts off slowly but ends in a rush.
Time is not something everyone has a lot of.
So make the best use of your time,
forget life's grime
and that it's full of crime.
Make time work for you.
Make time to play
and reading time.
Take time to dream,
it helps with self esteem.
Remember to laugh
and give much time to love
with a special one.
As with time,
you never know when
it will be your last.
You don't control time.
You will have to surrender to it.
Just try and manage it.
From the time you come into this world,
to when you leave this world,
you have no control over it:
time.

35 BEST FRIEND

My best friend,
you helped me mend.
So many times, I needed you
and didn't need to call.
You were already there,
straight talking at times,
when a level head is needed.
I should have known
and taken heed,
a true friend indeed.
Giving me strength
when it was most needed,
simply turning my frown
upside down
when acting the clown.
A true friend like you
never asks for anything back.
They just have your back.
I know with you
I can share anything
and you won't sing.
I'm proud to walk through life
all the stronger
with you by my side.
Thank you
my true friend.
A gift, if you like,
with me until the end.
My best friend.

36 DOGS

A flick of an ear, the tilting head
and the dog jumps on your bed
every morning.
The dog gets better treatment than the boyfriend.
Belly rubs galore,
while the boyfriend sits on the floor.
As you got off your chair
before he left the room it's in your chair and
you're no longer sitting there.
My home is your home
with that I know I'm never truly alone.
I'm glad I gave you a forever home.
Even when you've farted
and look at your own butt
then at me as if to say
"It wasn't me,
was it you?"
Dogs can lick down there, then stare and want to
lick your face,
as in, kiss you.
I sometimes despair
as they bark at you
until you take them for a walk,
it's their way to talk.
Standing proudly beside you
a stick between its teeth eager to please.
As you play with it,
just throw the stick and

they bring it back again.
Size doesn't matter,
or their colour or breed.
Loyal as anything
as they protect you.
Dogs are a person's best friend,
if a little wacky.

37 CATS

Cats loyalty is thin.
As long as you feed them
they stay within.
But easily led astray by
temptation of food,
or another cat looking for a fight,
or a good night.
Cats go out day and night,
sometimes giving you a fright,
as they pop in when you're sleeping.
No good ignoring
or pretend snoring.
They flick at your face
with gentle paws
then with claws.
"Get up and feed me, human!"
They see what you did,
they see you move an eyelid.
They will not go away.
Always getting their way.
There is no other way.
They sleep as much
as they are awake,
and play when it suits them
not you.
Getting a kiss is like having wet sandpaper rubbed
on your face.
Showing their love in so many different ways.

From that lick on the face,
to a cuddle in an awkward place.
Always getting in the way of something important,
even giving you a furball,
mouse and all,
but to hear them purr
is worth it all.

38 CAMPING

Tent full and brimming with family,
Yes, this is all good to thee.
Letting the moon and stars
be your lights as the campfire dies.
Caravanning or glamping are not for you.
You even like going on the plastic bucket-like loo.
The night creeps in,
eating crisps and drinking soda,
hot marshmallows
roasted on the fire.
Getting in the tent,
tucking yourself into
your sleeping bag
all nice and snug.
You say, "Who let all the bugs in?"
A lot of chatter, but soon all asleep.
A very early awakening,
as all the birds start chirping loudly,
and they don't shut up.
Not what you would call
a morning song,
sounds like every bird was having a ding-dong.
So you might as well get up,
even though it's still dark.
With the others stirring
it's breakfast time.
Not all chip in,
but still they're eating,

a bit unfair,
but you just sit back
in your camping chair.
You grin and bear.
Playing daytime games,
adults and children joining in.
Fun in the sun or clouds,
fresh air everywhere.
Camping is the life for you,
Relaxing, enjoying the outdoors.
Selfies galore,
you will camp a lot more

39 CHOCOLATE

Chocolate is sweet
making it too easy to eat.
Milk chocolate, dark chocolate
and white chocolate
only adds to my weight,
and that's just thinking about them.
My tease to please
is to slowly eat one piece
without eating any more.
"Does a whole bar count as one?"
I often ask myself.
Oh, how I love thee, chocolate.
You always smell heavenly.
You're intoxicating.
You shouldn't taste so good
and delicious,
it means I eat more of you than I should.
You're an addiction
I can't give up on,
and can't get myself
to get help for.
With little will power
you win every time.
Just that moment as it melts in my mouth and the
chocolate goes south
and touches my throat
is when I enjoy it the most.
Such heartache after a break-up,

chocolate can help lessen the pain.
No, really, it does.

40 BOOKS

Go on read one.
No, read a few.
Books are more than good for you.
They can take you to
another planet,
or just to a better place,
as you get lost in the pages.
So much going on
from cover to cover
as you travel through the ages
and back again.
A book can give hope
or just an escape.
From romance to a story on dance,
to a western or a sci-fi or a wonderland.
Opening a door
to the imagination,
all will have you in a trance,
all to be found inside a book.
There are lots of places
and new faces
to get to know.
Where they go
you will follow,
then know.
Learning all the time
with every page that's turned.

Go on, give reading a book
some time.
Get that yeaning,
burning,
overturning,
discerning
love of a good book.
Go on, open a book.
A real, physical book.
Be anything you want to be.
Plus,
you look good
holding a book
And no batteries to
recharge or replace.
Just saying.

41 SCHOOL

That summer flew by.
I didn't notice
it was gone in a
blink of an eye or two.
Back to school,
new year a beckoning.
New uniform,
new shoes,
new bag too.
Pens and pencils galore
but you always need more.
Hopefully new friends soon.
School.
It's all about learning,
it isn't disconcerting.
Teachers snap
but don't bite,
in fact, they're all right,
just helping you learn
to read and write
and do maths right.
Friends from the old school
mix with the new.
Lasting friendships can form from going to school.
Go, and be no-one's fool.
Ask any oldie.
They would rather
swap places with you.

To have another go at school.
Girlfriends and boyfriends
come and go,
just so you know,
school's rather social.

42 STRESS

Stress wears you down.
Gets to a point when you can't get air,
still not enough there.
Lungs are stretching, almost retching
Panic attack comes along and
takes its time to go.
as others try to comfort you.
If only they knew it was brought on by stress
to do with them.
Stress
leaves you feeling low
and washed out,
a living wreck
no doubt.
With no other release
it builds up once again.
Bitter, maybe twisted.
Is it jealousy?
Plain old guilt?
Maybe simply just too much to do?
Or is it you overthink things?
You need some help,
but none is forthcoming,
just empty good wishes.
Stress often goes by unnoticed
or mistaken,
a sickness that can kill,

for this here
is no pill to cure,
but to help if you procure.
Don't be ashamed in being you.
Get some help.
Put stress to one side,
and enjoy living life.

43 SCARS

Everyone has scars.
Scars are not just external,
but also internal.
Scars that are visible
show much pain outwardly,
but also reveal survival.
Bruises come and go, and yes, they hurt.
But to cut the skin, that leaves a scar you have to
live with,
as it leaves its mark
that may fade with time.
Each scar has a story to be told.
It means you have lived and survived, with scars,
laced like veins on your skin.
Some find scars sexy,
others find them hideous.
What is often not seen
is the cut that's within,
the pain you have gone through.
A false smile often covers
the inward scars
that don't or can't heal,
they just won't seal.
Still a living memory,
the pain is etched on the heart.
A scar is left behind
as the pain moved on.
You are just wanting

to be loved for who you are.
Scars are just what they are.
Don't be ashamed of them,
we all have them.

44 CUTS

I got a paper cut.
But I had the last laugh,
as I fed the paper to the shredder.
It won't be doing that again.
The next page nearly
had me the same.
In the shredder again.
An accidental cut will leave a scar,
a memory maybe too far.
A cut on purpose is with a purpose
as you cry silently out.
No one gets what it's about.
A fright that night,
don't cut no more,
put down the knife
and fight for life once more.
You can't blame it on
a cat scratch no more.
We've all seen it before,
cry out,
shout it out,
and help will be there.
Please cut no more,
someone that cares
is out there.
Give them time to find you,
and take away your pain,
or at least share its burden with you.

45 BIRTHDAYS

Birthdays come and go,
some seem so long ago.
You reach an age where
you don't care
anymore.
Don't sit and mope, you dope.
Get out there and mix.
Take a chance,
and you might find romance.
Don't let age hold you
back from happiness.
Take her to a dance.
Give her flowers.
Share a box of chocolates.
Just give her a chance,
after all it's your birthday.
Wishes can come true after all.
Share both birthdays together.
Let people in,
live again,
family and all.
A new soulmate forever more,
what a great birthday date.
And in the birthday card
she wrote
'love always, till the end of time'.
A happy end.

46 TEA

I made tea for two
as I was expecting your company,
but I'll have to make another brew
as I drank the one for you too.
One is never enough.
Weak or strong, as you like.
But strong is for me,
as I like to taste my tea.
A cold day, tea will warm it away.
If you get too hot, tea will
cool you down.
You get a tea when you
have a shock.
You get a tea if
something bad happens,
or something good happens.
Tea –
one of life's little pleasures
that doesn't cost the earth,
but puts most things right again.
There's breakfast tea,
elevenses tea,
dinner tea,
afternoon tea,
and teatime tea.
Don't forget evening tea
and then bedtime tea,
and many times, in-between,
you can never have enough tea
though it does make me pee a lot.

47 COFFEE

One coffee is never enough.
It takes two,
even if one's a takeaway.
Just make it strong.
Do I feel like cream, or take it black?
Frothy, or with chocolate on top?
Too many types to name,
choosing is a game
Just give me a white coffee to go.
Drink it on the way
to start your day
in a happy way.
When a room fills with that coffee aroma
it can sell houses
or even build houses.
At the end of the day there is nothing better than a
hot coffee,
and a coffee flavoured kiss.
It leaves its mark on a table
or counter top, but
a ring of coffee is no problem.
Finish the coffee,
simply put the mug on top
and the ring has gone.
No more coffee rings,
it is a coffee table after all.
Until morning sings,
when washing up begins,

and the mark is wiped away
ready for a fresh one that day.
A new stain is only one coffee away.

48 BEER

I would drink beer with my dear,
no fear.
I'd even smear beer on a cashier,
and lick it off,
as long as I got to drink my beer.
I've had many an affair with beer,
taken it everywhere near and far.
Why look for happiness when it's right there in
beer?
A pint or two,
or a few,
it's up to you.
It's beer o'clock.
If you want to make me
even happier,
a cold pint, then maybe
just one more.
Go on, dear, and get me a beer,
you can have one too.
Or you can have mine, dear,
we have more.
Then again, there's always
home brew.
What say you?
The saying you want to hear:
'I've got you a beer in'.
As you walk in the pub,
You are filled with cheer,
soon to be beer.

49 WINE

Divine a perfect word to
describe wine.
Taken from the vine
to make perfect wine.
You don't need to drink wine
to get drunk.
Drink it to enjoy it.
Don't overdo it
then throw it up.
What's the point in doing that?
Sip it, taste it,
don't neck it.
Don't whine about wine.
Go out and dine with wine.
Red or white,
sweet or dry.
Just depends on what you're eating.
Or buck the trend,
and have what colour you want instead.
Just say please.
Wine in a box, ready to pour.
Is it a good thing or a bad thing?
All I know is I want more.
Is the glass half full or half empty?
Fill it up, then who cares?

50 TOAST

Toast for breakfast or for tea;
it's the way to go for me.
I like toast when its lightly toasted, just turning
brown.
Then again, I like toast if it's very well done and
dark brown.
If it's burnt I won't waste it,
I'll eat it,
scrape off the black
and it's good to go.
When asked on different
levels of brown
I just frown.
It's all lost on me.
I just want toast.
There are cereals and fruit to be had,
but I'd rather have toast instead.
With crusts? Without crusts? A question to ponder.
For me, leave the crusts on please.
When asked, I have toast as it comes,
only leaving crumbs
behind as I eat and go.
Nothing here to show.
In a hurry, toast on the go.
Marg or butter,
eggs or beans or both.
Jam or spam,
knife and fork or hands.

The choice is yours:
hot, warm or cold.
Toast.

51 FOOTBALL

Taking to the pitch is everyone's favourite team.
Football players kick and scream
Taking aim at the goal
or players on the other team.
Some fine specimens of athletes,
some not.
Running all day
tackling away -
well, ninety minutes.
They act as though it was all day.
Some players have skills to perform,
sending the crowd wild,
then comes along a special one
with all the tricks.
We all like that.
But some are like clowns,
and know no bounds.
But if they give the ball away,
they can go down
with a frown
in the hope the ref blows his whistle.
Sometimes it goes against them and they get a
yellow card.
Other times they get a free kick.
Some call it cheating.
Some call it 'taking one for the team'
or 'time wasting'.
So not always the best team wins.

It's win by whatever means.
That's why football is a great game,
a team game,
unpredictable,
as it should be.
Football.

52 THE BEACH

A day at the beach
is a peach.
Pack the bucket and spade
and windbreak.
Picnic too,
that I will share with you.
Touch the sand with your toes.
Crunch the sand as you
scrunch your toes.
Grainy yet fine, it's holiday time.
Let's build a fine sandcastle.
Bucket and spade get to work.
The castle grows as the sand goes,
then there has to be a moat.
Off to the edge of the sea you go,
the sea is cool as it gets your toes wet.
In and out it goes,
as you watch the white waves breaking,
just out of reach.
You prefer to stay on the beach.
Moat filled, it's a thrill to eat
your picnic on the beach,
with sand between your toes,
a sneeze almost putting
sand up your nose
as you wipe the sneeze away.
Time to find a nice shell
to keep for that sea smell.

It's time to go,
the shell will remind me
when we get home
of the day at the beach,
along with the many pictures we took,
good memories made every time.

53 THE SEA

The sea can be serene.
A true thing of beauty,
a must to be seen.
But like us it has its bad days
When it turns grey, then black.
There's no looking back
on that.
The sound of the sea floating by,
with the waves crashing nearby,
is like one of life's lullabies.
A dolphin swims alongside
a pleasure boat.
The sea looks so clear
with its near crystal water,
pushing sand and shells ashore.
Fish swimming out to sea
staying out of the way.
Seaweed, the sea's flowers, waving away.
Children dancing in the waves near to shore,
following the rhythm of the sea
as it flows in and out.
Dads, with their trousers rolled up.
Fishing boats, pleasure boats,
anything that floats,
the sea plays with them.
Dolphins to whales to tiny fishes
all live within.
The sea holds so many secrets.

Beautiful, enchanting, yet deadly
if misused
and abused
by humans.
Keep it clean!

54 CLOUDS

White clouds floating by
with a lovely blue background sky.
Find a hill,
lay and chill,
watching the clouds floating by.
Making out patterns;
first a clown, then a dog,
followed by a frog.
Just watch the clouds float by.
They never sit still,
always on the move,
helped by the wind of course.
Grey clouds arrive, and rain ensues,
almost follows you
as you run for cover.
The now black clouds pin you down with a frown
taking over the sky,
thunder and lightning abound
hitting the ground
and anything nearby.
You stand and watch in awe
as the clouds seem angry,
unlike before.
Clouds are such wonderous things,
wouldn't you want to explore?
To be amongst the clouds,
to touch them,
then to pass through them

and look from above.
One day we will all be able to touch the sky
and float on by,
following the clouds.
Not to skydive or parachute by,
but to really fly.
Never say never.
One day, we'll see you floating by,
as technology will allow.
Touch a cloud for me,
as I'm too old.

55 SELFIE

Taking a selfie
seems the modern way to go.
Making sure everyone can see
with no privacy.
They even put it on a stick
to take the selfie
as if another had taken it.
With their pouting lips
and hands on hips
in the usual look-at-me pose.
So much self-love,
me in every other pose.
Or what they are having for tea,
often at someone else's pain,
seems to be a selfie gain.
Turn the phone and
shoot yourself,
and someone's pain behind you.
Selfie accomplished
Once, we took pictures of what was in front of us,
now it's all about taking them of us.
You take a tumble and fall,
you take a selfie.
You make yourself look a fool,
you take a selfie.
All will judge, rightly or wrongly,
as you put them on social media,
in competition to get

more hits than your friends.
Just remember to look behind you,
in case they can see more of you
than you intended,
be it a mirror
or a reflection of your lower region on a shiny
surface.
It might be the wrong face giving the impression.

56 HOME

Home is
not just walls and a roof.
Home is where you are
loved and give love
with friends and family.
There are family pictures hanging.
This home has
tell-tale marks of little ones,
toys not strewn but in place.
A tidy home
where it's nice to roam,
quiet and safe.
Lots of love in this one.
Children playing
and music quietly playing
just loud enough to hear,
it makes for good cheer.
Your home will shelter you
from storms or the sun,
or hiding from that
so-called special one
(after you found another one).
My home is built for
love and dreams.
Never extremes.
Down a wee country lane
is the house for me,
cute as can be,

quaint as you like,
very picture-like.
With a large open fireplace
burning bright
to always welcome thee.
You put on your shoes and walk out the door,
but your love stays there evermore
waiting for you to open that door
once more.
A happy home.

57 MAKEUP

Makeup done right
takes away a fright,
but done wrong
can give a fright to everyone.
Are you putting it on to hide from the real you?
Like war paint to take away the prying eyes.
By looking fierce to the eye,
does it hide the times you cry,
letting makeup hide further tears?
Do you put it on to please others?
Or for you?
To make you look good and feel good?
If so, I don't blame you.
Confidence given.
But remember,
there is always beauty within
as well as on the outside.
Go out makeup-free,
what a great sight.
Nothing covered,
it's just you,
the real you.
But, if you need it to feel confident, then do
put on blusher and lipstick
and feel confident and free.
Just be who you are,
not who others want or
expect you to be.

Everyone is beautiful
in their own way.
Don't put on makeup to
hide from yourself.
Use it to set yourself free.
You're beautiful, believe me.

58 UNDER MY BED

I would take a peek under my bed,
but I wouldn't like
what I would find.
Probably a monster of some kind.
The one that eats my socks,
one at a time as they
go missing at washing time.
Maybe food it left behind
is lurking under there.
Some things,
you just can't tell what they are,
or even were,
they all lurk under there.
Probably some underwear,
that soon will walk out of there
on its own
and make you swoon.
Plus, it smells of old socks
and like dad's shoes
under there.
Mum says I'm silly.
Dad says I'm a Silly-Billy,
but I know there's *something*
under there.
Every time I move
and a spring goes twang,
I think the monster is under there.
I'm sure I hear it breathing

now and again.
I'm worried it's feeding time
and it wants me.
Maybe the monsters aren't real,
but only in my head,
not under my bed,
but I'd rather you look, instead.

59 AEROPLANES

Apprehensive at first,
then full of excitement
as you enter the aeroplane.
Sitting looking at the tarmac below,
then it moves.
It turns and the engines roar,
and you start to climb.
You can't see the ground any more
just clouds all around.
You look, but don't see the stars.
They are just out of reach at night.
The stars look bright
out of the little window.
Aeroplanes seen from below,
a few blinking lights
on its wings and tail
to say it's there,
not a shooting star.
It's an aeroplane up there.
During the day it can be seen,
small, but up there,
as the aeroplane flies by.
Contrails left behind,
the only reminder
an aeroplane was even there.

60 TRAINS

A train journey is full of
wonder and woe,
as the wrong leaves on its rails
can halt a train.
Then again, snow does the same.
On the train
going to work for the day,
a few hours later
coming home again,
just another commuter.
Trains are fast and fun
when it's not work time,
and you can even sleep on some.
The trains in the future
will hover,
no bother.
They won't need rails anymore,
go anywhere, anytime,
that will be the future train.
It will run in snow,
on snow,
above the snow,
and rain,
even of the heaviest kind.
No human drivers needed,
electronics controlling it instead.
Always on time
and no leaves will bother it again.
Travel by train.

61 UNIFORM

School uniform.
Soldier's uniform.
All must conform.
But all look good to me.
A police officer, a fire fighter.
Some uniforms are there to protect
and not just look good.
A nurse:
now there's someone
who helps to mend every one,
wearing a uniform all day, performing in a special
healing way.
When you put on your uniform
for the first time
you get nervous
but when you get there
you are just the same as all the rest,
well-dressed
in a uniform, neat and clean.
Smelling of laundry soap,
looking smart, feeling smart,
that's what a uniform does for you.
I wonder these days
if jeans and a t-shirt or polo shirt
count as a uniform?
It seems to be the way it goes.
A uniform makes you
stand out in a crowd,

loud and proud.
Yes, a uniform does it for me.

62 SUNDAY ROAST

Family getting together for a
Sunday roast.
A toast,
and the meat gets cut,
be it chicken or pork,
gammon or turkey,
beef or lamb or a vegetarian meal.
As you wait to fill your plate
you salivate
in anticipation.
The Sunday roast is
a family tradition
that's slowly getting lost to progress
as families spend longer apart,
as time moves on.
Roast potatoes and
Yorkshire pudding,
meat and veg on the side,
gravy poured delicately over.
As it brings the family closer,
as they talk,
not screen talk,
but real words are spoken,
while smelling the aroma
of what family time is all about.
Then it's time to tuck in,
enjoying all that's before you
as it's dinner time.

Put your phones and tablets aside
and enjoy the
Sunday roast once more.
Don't let it fade away,
invite the family today.

63 SHAVE

Shave and buck the trend
to become one of the hairy kind.
Shave your sideburns,
make that moustache fade as you shave away.
Rub the cream on your face
and shave with a blade
like the old days.
Or electric shave and have no cream.
Or, you could shave with
a safety razor and gel
your way to
looking and smelling swell.
Shaving gives you an uplift
on a sad or boring day.
It's always been that way.
You feel better after a shave.
Show and tell.
Some have hair on their head
fading away
so choose to shave the rest away.
Sometimes in a vain way,
others as it's needed that way.
Some treat a shave like an operation,
as they skirt around
different shapes of hair
that they choose
to wear on their face or head.
A little nick here,

a little cut there,
could ruin a wedding day.
So, a fresh blade,
and a careful shave
on that special day
as little squares of torn toilet paper
don't look so good
in your wedding photobook,
as they cover you
when a shave goes too far.

64 HOSPITAL

Hospitals:
you can tell
by the cleanliness smell,
by the waiting rooms
full of the unwell.
In there for rest,
but it's noisier than at home.
Given a gown
that doesn't go around
and you're left
showing your bare behind.
From taking x-rays
to removing toenails,
anything that entails blood.
They do it all.
Visiting time costs the most,
having to park nice and close,
taking flowers or fruit
to a friend or a loved one
who need it the most.
Finding them on a ward
or in a private room.
Lying so still,
sheets pulled high.
From the survivors we hear the most,
tears and laughter
and whoops, and "Oh, yeah!"
until a nurse tells you

to keep it down.
The other side, the smile is
upside down,
and the tears are not for happiness.
Unfortunately, this is how life goes,
and death follows.
Hospitals, as it goes, try to help you.
They do all they can.
You go in,
you may not come out.
That's what hospitals are all about.

65 MIST

A rolling mist covers the ground
as people walk the town
unable to look down.
Waiting for the breeze to make the ground appear
again.
Then the mist will lift and roll away
as fast as it came down.
The mist has an aroma of its own.
Dampness, yet fruitfulness,
and some happiness,
though some naughtiness.
A thin veiled mist
blankets the village.
Blink and you will miss
as amongst the mist
things go amiss.
Certain people
take advantage of the situation.
The mist hangs just above the lake,
looking majestic and kind.
So delicate,
all the trees swaying
in the arriving breeze.
As water droplets fall,
a reminder of
what the mist left behind.
As everything gleams or glows,
sometimes it's a shame it has to go.

66 SPLINTER

Splinters can get anywhere.
Some places you don't want others to know.
Certainly, some places tweezer shouldn't go,
but they must.
That's a splinter too far.
For some,
a pain extreme.
They get under your skin,
Irritate.
You just daren't ask
how they got them there.
You can see them,
certainly, feel them.
Normally they tend to make
a bigger hole as they come out
than when they went in.
Some splinters you can't see,
those invisible ones.
Oh, how you can feel
as you touch that part of skin,
you know there is a splinter within, and under your
skin,
and you want it out.
Under a nail is extreme,
hard to get out.
You want to suck them out,
but a splinter in the tongue
is just wrong.
So you just fish away with a needle
the old-fashioned way,

until they show a tail,
then in you sail
with the tweezers.
There it is, the little bleeder.
You take a breather,
as there is always another splinter to go.

67 TALK

Some people talk too much.
Others, not enough.
From romantic pillow talk
to talking
whilst walking
in the park.
They are lucky people
who can talk.
Others just don't get the time
or the right time
or the right person to talk to.
Always talk if you can.
Talking dirty in someone's ear
can be effective
anywhere
for getting
or suggesting
what you want.
Then there's the person in the street
who simply talks too much,
or a neighbour
who catches you
as you try to creep out again,
with so much to say
about anything and everything
from football to
what was on the big screen.
A zip wouldn't go amiss.

Never go silent,
just talk to me.
Not about me,
to my face.
I am always willing to listen.
Do you want to talk about it?

68 LIBRARY

A great place to meet,
or go alone.
Friendly, always full of people with a glow,
knowing they know
they will be left alone to
indulge in what they can't at home.
Or even to take home to finish;
so much knowledge.
Written to be read,
not computer fed.
Feel a book, read a book,
and best of all
it doesn't need charging or batteries to fulfil its
task.
The library takes you
anywhere you want to go.
Into space, underground,
to airspace, and a flight
that comes home.
Mixing with fairies
and giant dragons,
or old westerns.
Some that will scare you,
or a mystery to solve.
You can even listen to books,
or it teaches you
without a teacher before you.
Learning a new culture or

a new language.
Go on, take it home,
read it alone.
Lose yourself,
transform yourself.
Put a smile on your face.
You can do it all at the library,
just remember to bring your library card.

69 ROSE

A rose in a field can whisper to all
as it sways gently in the breeze, almost as a tease.
From its aroma to its colour
to its beauty, a rose is
a win for all.
A rose is sometimes a
double-edge blade.
Careful how you tread
as given a chance it will prick you
instead of you picking it.
Now you bleed red,
the colour of the rose you chose.
A dozen red roses show
a love from within.
Even friendship,
or just comfort.
It's all about the thought given
with all your dreams coming true.
A single rose
shows a love being given.
A red rose is the same colour
as a heart
that's why it's best to be given,
be it for love or friendship.
Gift a heaven-sent rose today,
let it lead the way.
You get a smile with a rose
Everyone knows.

70 TULIP

Tulips like to grow
in a row.
Not alone.
Soaking up the sun's rays,
and soaking up the rain.
Holding them in its cupped leaves,
taking a sip to the very last drop.
Tulips bring you the sunshine
and warmth
so you can breathe again.
Bringing the bright light back again.
Brighter skies as the tulips rise,
given as a great surprise.
Tulips melt the heart,
a visual treat in the street,
as you walk by gardens
full of rows of tulips.
Visually appealing,
with them any colour goes.
A tulip's life is to make
everything around it
beautiful and serene.
True friends are like flowers
that never fully fade
when squashed in a book,
memory took,
a keepsake.
Give a tulip or two today.

71 MARRIAGE

Marriage the bond of
love.
With give and take,
and respect,
to share the good and bad.
With trust involved,
everything has to evolve,
grow together in everyway.
Blessed, with rice and
confetti thrown.
Hoping there are no embarrassing speeches.
The first dance as a married pair.
Everyone has chance to stare.
Even your second cousins are there.
Never hold back from saying
you love your partner.
Remember to show
how much you care.
Walk proudly hand-in-hand
to show everyone
your love of togetherness.
Remember romance.
Sometimes there are times
when you need to look through
your partner's eyes
to realise what's there.
No argument then,
no hidden secrets, tell all.

It's worth it in the end,
everything can mend.
Understand your partner's unconditional love for
you.
You can get through it all,
laugh it all off together,
as you grow old together.
Just continue to fall in love
everyday.
Love gives you life,
problems shared.
Marriage does that for you:
caring and sharing,
a vow worth taking,
marriage.

72 WRITERS

Words, swimming in my head.
I put them on paper instead.
The voice from within won't silence
until it's written down.
A writer seems to have
a short memory span.
Their best ideas and
words and phrases
come when there is no pen
or paper to show.
When they get paper,
where did the words go?
Often an elusive person,
hiding themselves,
drowning themselves in coffee,
getting lost in a character created.
To write, there is the need to read.
This has to be done,
so, leave them be,
underneath that tree,
silent and alone,
but in reality,
they are lost in a world in a book.
Certainly not alone;
just where they want to be.
At home they sit,
pen in hand, paper laid out,
ready to go.

Then coffee calls,
and writing stalls.
Sitting staring at a blank page,
staring back at thee is the writers' thinking pose.
Waiting for writer's block
to unlock
and the pen to work again.
As the words flow
in a cascade of letters
hoping to cover the page,
whether you're writing a novel
or poetry instead,
or homework on the bed,
writers write to be read.

73 POETS

Poets:
some like to rhyme all the time.
Others some of the time.
Some none of the time.
From fairy tales,
to poems about gales.
Poetry brings it all home to thee.
Poetry is fitting together of words that matter,
need to be said.
Good or bad.
Bringing expressions of emotions
from notions.
Creating short phrases,
placing feelings.
Spontaneous, or simultaneous.
Free words, no story to maintain
or restrain the flow.
Comparisons to nonsense.
A poem is as short or as long as it flows,
not a word more.
It finishes itself
using a metaphor, or four or more.
Simile abounds,
it's all poetry to me.

74 WEEKEND

The week's end has arrived,
none too soon.
Weekend has arrived.
I have no place to be, which suits me
Coffee, a good book,
some chocolates alongside.
Plenty of me-time ahead.
Saturday comes and
seems to fly by,
way too quick and slick.
Sunday, my real rest day,
when if I could, I'd lie in bed
all day.
Or go to the park for the day.
Maybe a swim that day for pleasure, not for
fitness.
A leisurely stroll is about
as far as I would like to go.
Maybe a two-day weekend
could or should
be stretched to a three-day weekend,
even if it was just for me.
I deserve it.
The next weekend
it's time to party again,
Just the Saturday night;
Sunday is all about me again
as I take the car

for a spin to the beach.
Picnic on the beach.
Found a spot
amongst the hordes and surfboards.
I sat taking in the sun's rays
with a good book for the day.
Girlfriend by my side,
she is reading her book again.
We hear nothing around
as though there was no sound,
no children running screaming by,
no seagull taking flight,
no radio nearby.
Our books take us away from this.
A quick drive, and back home again,
weekend over again,
shame.
Nearly spoiled by it
coming to an end,
but I get to do it all again
at the next weekend.
It just needs to hurry itself along.

75 GRANDCHILDREN

Grandchildren, full of smiles
all the while.
Silly games with me
of course, treats galore,
and then some more.
Out in the garden we all go,
where we hope they let go
of their everlasting energy.
Always asking questions,
inquisitive to say the least.
Little hands and paint everywhere,
handprints visible for all to see.
Later, they choose a book
and it's story time.
A nice quiet time
if they sit still and listen,
then some television.
Too young for me,
I choose to read.
At least it's a rest for me,
then mum and dad come along.
A hug if I'm lucky.
A child from my child.
A joy to see.
At least we can give them back,
we're thankful for that.
But it's nice to be a grandparent.
We can be serious
or act silly and get away with it.

76 AUNTIE

Auntie with a heart so pure
who I truly adore.
You unselfishly gave to me,
Auntie, you spent quality time
with me,
believed in me.
Taught me so much,
talked about anything
without getting in a huff.
My auntie can keep a secret
like a sister would or should.
My auntie always knows
what to say and do,
and advises accordingly.
Giving comfort or cheer,
or a telling off too.
She also gives encouragement
when needed.
Auntie you are a friend indeed
to me.
Oh, how I love thee.
I should tell you this
more often
so you don't feel forgotten.
A special one,
especially as we grow older.
Now you are a great-auntie too,
don't forget me.

77 UNCLE

An uncle: a true family friend.
Always there to defend.
When I was young he'd tickle me.
Now he plays ball with me.
My uncle always has time for me.
He feels like a friend
when I'm in need.
Almost a big brother to me.
Happy or sad,
you always encourage me,
you laugh with me,
yet protect me.
Often funny and full of cheer
for all to hear.
As a party guest you are always welcome,
jokes galore
and so much more.
You guided me through life,
from a tot to a youth to an adult too,
always good advice from you.
I look up to you, Uncle.

78 BROTHER

A brother is someone you love,
then hate,
then love again.
A brother will back you
if you're right, and
sometimes when you're wrong,
just to get along.
Always with you,
you stole my toys
then gave them back again.
Some broken,
some not.
Stole my comics
then returned them,
no longer pristine as they should have been.
Shared good times,
some bad times,
certainly, some sad times.
Laughed together,
cried together.
Fought together.
There were many squabbles
and fights galore
but it meant I only loved you more,
just maybe not at the time.
As we age,
we see each other less
but we remain close by telephone.

As a brother you are swell,
just don't tell.
I'm proud to have you as a brother,
I love you, brother.

79 SISTER

A sister so loud and proud.
There will always be drama days.
One day they will hug you,
the next day they will hate you,
most of the time bug you,
but always love you.
Tears to wipe away as things don't go their way,
times she wishes you went away,
times you wished she
would go away.
But the next day best friends again.
So many days
where it was normal to fight like cats and dogs.
Yet she knows how you are feeling.
Understanding when others aren't
getting you.
Sharing an unbreakable bond.
Always remembers birthdays and dates.
On a sad day,
you turn it to a happy day.
But still,
you have to have it your way.
Many times, we shared,
as we laughed or cried.
A sister you will always be,
and a friend to me, my sister.

80 CAKES

Cakes pull people in from afar
by aroma or sight.
They can't keep away.
Cakes. A way to many a heart.
Cakes so sweet and never bittersweet.
There's chocolate or vanilla
or strawberry,
with icing on top.
Butter icing in between.
All taste good to me.
A multi-tier cake or a cupcake,
not forgetting birthday cakes
and wedding cakes.
A cake is a tease,
one piece is never enough to please.
So take a bigger piece.
A cake in a box never lasts long.
It's a tease that needs to be eased,
so you wipe your finger
where you hope no one will see.
No candles on top of a cake,
a new face is born.
One candle soon comes along.
As you age, the cake needs to grow
to hold enough candles to match you
which can only be a good thing.
More cake, please.

81 BIRDS

A song from a bird
is speaking without saying words,
simply music making,
breath-taking.
Listening is our pleasure.
Almost a thank you
for the food and water
we put out.
Just wish we knew
what they were talking about.
All from a bird so small,
feathers to keep them warm.
Some are bright and cheerful,
others dull and practical.
You have it all:
a nest built of twigs
and hair so fine and fair
to line it all,
in a tree standing so tall,
or a hedge just off the edge,
in a hole in the ground
they can be found,
laying eggs
so young ones abound.
Worms have to go further.
Oh, birds how I envy you,
with your wings and flight
and freedom of the sky.

82 TREES

Trees short or tall
or bushy, we need them all.
From their beauty comes oxygen,
nature's cleaners and providers.
Trees tell us when seasons change.
From bare limbs
to leaves covering everywhere.
Then there are evergreens,
showing colour all year round.
I remember climbing an oak tree,
so tall when I was small.
Lucky I didn't fall.
Just to see what can be seen
from the very top,
a place where the birds live,
work and play.
A supplier of food
to the birds and other animals.
The same with insects
and all protection from above.
A resting place
for the birds of prey,
as the other birds have flown away.
Supplier of the wood to build with
and paper to write on and read from.
We need to treat them right,
don't give them a fright
by cutting them down,

unless it's to re-plant new ones again.
A tree spreads its branches
and reaches out for us
in nature
to help us.
So let's help each tree
and let them be.

83 PIES

A pie makes you salivate
as you look at it.
Not just the smell of it,
though the aroma draws you in
as it lures you in for a piece.
But one piece is never enough
as you stuff your face.
Another piece is no disgrace.
No one is looking,
go on, one more piece.
Apple pie to pumpkin pie,
to a meat pie,
hot or cold,
they are a staple to us all.
With lovely pastry, soft or crumbly,
and a filling to die for,
so divine.
Go on, enjoy your pie.
Visitors come and go,
pies went well.
Not a crumb left behind.
Nothing more satisfying
than seeing an empty pie dish.
You just wish there was more.

84 STARS

When I look up at night
and see the stars doing their thing,
I wonder what could have been.
Every star for every wish I've had,
with so many left over.
That's why there are so many
out there.
So much left undone.
I should be a more decisive one.
Younger ones
think stars hang on strings
as they glisten away.
Oh, to shine as bright as the stars
I stare at every night.
If it's clear enough,
like decisions in life.
It's not always clear
enough to see them
and not sure what path to take
with no star to shine the way.
If you're lucky you will get to see
a shooting star,
then you'll know where you are.
No mistake,
shining down at you
like a million eyes
as they twinkle away.
Watching us from above,

as we watch them from below.
Are we alone?

85 MOON

The moon is beautiful and has it all.
It reflects light on us to see by.
Enough light to cry by,
and laugh by.
And to catch a crook by.
A friendly moon.
For some that work nights
the moon is your sun
and you like it in full bloom
to light the way and your day.
The morning almost comes too soon,
so good day moon.
Time to hide away as the
sun comes up for the day.
Everyone must try to walk silently
under the light of a bright full moon.
Invigorating, mind blowing,
fulfilling their thoughts,
the moon puts on rare shows
with an eclipse.
Then the special one:
there is the blood moon to look upon.
Not many years until we all can visit the moon
on a day trip.
Personally, I can't wait to explore.
Can you?

86 SAD

Don't be too sad.
Weep to get over it. Don't stand still.
You will always remember me,
and I'll always watch over thee.
My regret is watching over you
when you're so sad,
and being unable to hug you
or comfort you in any way.
But remember:
I still love you.
Your heart holds it all,
so, no need to be sad at all.
Don't let memories fade away,
remember our time to the last day.
Please smile like before,
with a glint in your eyes
to take that sad look away
as life moves on.
I see you on my funeral day,
silently standing, not listening
to people's words,
and songs your mind couldn't hear.
Crying, not taking it all in.
Just thinking of
what could have been.
We hugged, and I held on
till my dying day, my last hour.
It had to come, you knew that,

but it didn't make it any easier
as we never got to do this and that.
Our list was incomplete,
makes you so sad.
Pick one and do it,
and think of me.
Close your eyes
and I'm there with you
always.
I pass this to you
while you're sleeping.

87 HAPPY

When you're happy,
standing in the rain doesn't dampen anything.
Happy can be losing yourself
in a good book,
happy to have great friends and friendships
and happy to have
the silence around you
when you need it most?
Happy is coming home to a pet
to cuddle up to.
Happy is when a partner does things for you
without asking.
Happy makes the stories
people want to read.
Are there ever any happy endings?
Don't kiss me so hard,
it knocks me down again
as you say goodbye.
Maybe we should enjoy
the happy start,
and middle,
and ignore
the unhappy ending.
See, you can't buy happy,
only some happy times.
Unless you find the right one,
then live happy as can be
as the story unfolds.

You make the ending,
so make it a happy ending.

88 SLEEPING

I love to watch you sleeping,
your eyes twitching
through closed eyelids.
Listening to your breathing,
sometimes you whistle
whilst sleeping and breathing.
Even your snoring isn't boring.
Wrapping yourself in the duvet whilst sleeping
can be a little bit freezing
when you move
and get out of the duvet.
I tuck you in again,
tucking in your little sticky-out feet again and again,
and start watching you
sleeping once more,
hoping when you're dreaming,
you dream of me,
of us.
Always think of me
as I do you.
It helps me sleep
just to know you're asleep
next to me.
Upon awakening,
I hope sleeping has re-charged you.
Let the previous day's worries
fade away,
to be awesome some more.

From our first time
to our last time of sleeping together,
you will always be my
sleeping beauty.
I love waking up next to you
more than I love sleeping.

89 LIGHTS

City lights seen from above
look so appealing,
but upon arriving
it's not all that.
Just lots of lights,
Twinkling in shop windows,
house windows.
And streetlamps
lighting up the way.
The odd passing car,
that's all they are
with colour added
when near not far.
The green, amber and red
of a traffic light set.
The torch light of a dog walker.
These all add together
and look so much more from afar.
When near a light, what do you see
but a moth or three?
Light draws you in,
whoever and whatever you are.
Lighthouses swing their light beams near and far,
to keep the ships from
shallow waters and harm.
Some cities never sleep.
There is always a light on there,
back up the hill

for me to watch from above,
from the shadows,
without a light on me.
Just watch the lights twinkle away.

90 PUDDLES

As the storm passes away,
puddles made by the rain,
right by the over-flowing drain,
or down the muddy lane.
All there to jump in.
Puddles mean fun for everyone,
young or old.
Be bold and jump on in.
Just remember to be wearing boots.
Watch the big puddles
as the ducks go wading.
That's when you know for sure
it has been raining.
Birds bathe in the puddles
you once stepped in.
When the murky waters clear
its nature's bath.
The sun comes out
and the drying starts.
Bye bye, puddles no more
until it rains again.
If people won't step in
or over a puddle for you,
don't cross a river to be with them.
You won't like them when you
truly get to know them.
Remember that.
Puddles.

91 SPEED

Speed,
and the need to win
go hand in hand.
Not necessarily a good thing
but often a done thing.
For some, speed is addiction.
Don't let it become an affliction.
Two legs versus four legs -
four wins.
Twice as good as two legs, it seems.
If you are in control you are not at maximum
speed.
If all about you is shaking and falling apart,
and you're losing control,
then you are at maximum safe speed.
Do not exceed.
It won't end prettily.
With the speed of thought
you slow down to do it all again.
A speed record is to be broken,
whether on ground,
on sea, even under the sea,
or in the air,
done with flair,
but with safety there.

92 SEAGULL

You see the shadow, when you walk,
of the seagull up above.
Watching it swoop and dive
then fly back up above.
It gives you a buzz.
It means it's the season
and the beach beckons.
Holidays, I reckon.
You see a seagull ride the swell
as you take in that sea smell.
Confident and brash
you see the seagulls dash
as a chip is dropped on the floor.
A lady looking distraught,
one or more seagulls
make the dash, then
a swoop and whoosh as the wings
fly in from above.
The chips didn't stand a chance and
that blooming seagull
nicked my ice-cream
as I stand and scream.
Then a lady screams
as she's covered in something
that's not ice-cream
dropped from the seagull now far above.
"At least I didn't get that,"
I thought.
It was rather a lot.

93 HATS

A hat for me is happy as can be.
It means the sun's out
and I intend going out.
A hat for some hides so much.
A hat can change anyone.
Wear a hat for warmth.
Wear a hat to be model of the month.
Wear a hat for confidence.
Wear a hard hat to protect you.
It's not a fashion statement,
but a safety statement.
Sirens go off and the watch is off
as the firemen don their
helmets
with a fire beckoning
for them to attend.
Or wear a hat for play,
becoming anyone you want.
Be a pirate or a witch for the day
when you play dress-up.
Be a magician for the day,
pull a rabbit out of the hat
before you put it on.
Grandad, and his flat cap
is his hat of the day, and every day.
He still tips his hat to this day
when a lady passes his way.
Just being polite.

Don't leave your hat upside down,
or a cat will
make it a bed for the day.
Which one will you wear today?

94 CLOTHES

Wearing clothes
hides the fact you're bare underneath.
Clothes keep you warm.
Wear clothes to be in fashion
and nice and trendy,
or wear clothes for protection.
You can wear clothes to pose,
or no clothes if you dare.
Jeans tight and sexy,
with a pair of knee high boots,
does it for me.
When clothes are washed and aired
they smell like they should be.
Sometimes, when you awaken,
and no time taken,
you put on your clothes,
but the labels show
this is not the way to go.
Clothes lines can tell a lot
about what's going on
and coming off
if you know what I mean.
Even though they look divine
some leave you red faced,
as a lot of it is lace.
Certainly not work clothes
which are all hot and itchy,
worn for practicality not fashion.

Losing weight is great,
as it means you need
new clothes again.
Bit of a pain,
but what a nice pain.
Nice new clothes.

95 WINDOWS

Windows clean and bright
for you to see out.
Also, windows can be seen in.
Dirty windows hide what's in.
Storm windows keep
the weather out.
Shuttered windows to hide behind.
Sometimes as you look
out of the window
you look into another window
and see something you don't want to.
But also, a pleasing sight can be seen sometimes,
as long as the window is clean.
Looking out of a window to dream
allows you to get lost in the dream,
away from what could have been,
for a little while it would seem.
The wrong people
love a window left open,
so shut before leaving.
Even a cat can get in the smallest gap of any
window.
Maybe a cat-burglar
can do the same.
You never know who's watching.
Switch the light off from within,
and look out of the window at what's around at
night.

It might surprise you,
even frighten you,
with who's stalking about.
Blinds and curtains curtail vision
if closed fully
with just a little gap at the
edge or middle.
I'll be seeing you
will you see me?

96 DOORS

Open doors let you in.
Closed doors stop you from
getting in.
A door slammed in your face
can leave you in disgrace,
and your face a disgrace,
as blood drips down from a
squashed nose.
A screen door is not secure,
but says keep out,
I'm trying to keep the insects out.
You still need to knock to get let in.
A door stands so tall and proud
or small and sweet.
Just remember to wipe your feet.
You feel safer on the other side of a locked door.
A creaking door can be frightening,
especially if accompanied by lightening
as a storm passes,
but it's only your roommate
turning up late again.
Briefly you wonder where she's been.
Back to dreaming as you feel safe
at home.
A mother can dread opening a bedroom door.
Will it be smelly
with a worn sock left on the telly?
Socks peeling from the ceiling,

old cold pizza half eaten.
Underwear thrown everywhere,
or will the door lead to a
nice and clean bedroom
where is everything hidden?
All the excess,
a door to the closet is all
that's in-between.
Best leave that door shut.
Worst thing is standing
outside of the house
and the wind picks up and slam goes the door
with the key on the table indoors,
and windows locked.
Best keep a spare key to your door
somewhere
now you know how secure
your door is
as you just stand there
waiting.

97 GIFTS

Don't wait for Christmas or birthday.
Gift a present anytime.
You can hand deliver, or have it sent.
It's still money well spent.
A gift can be a new life.
Or a new wife.
A gift for love.
A gift for sorrow.
Money that's needed,
it tells it all
about the person giving,
what a generous soul.
Gift your heart today
to the one you want to spend the rest of your life
with.
Giving a gift to a teacher
as you leave,
simply a nice thank you
for all their help.
It isn't about size or amount,
a gift is simply about giving.
A small gift can grow, just sow it.
Let it grow.
Remember also you are a gift if given in friendship.
One of the most precious gifts is time.
Use it wisely or lose it.
You have to spend time carefully,
a gift worthy of receiving.
Just remember it.

98 STORM

A storm warning is given.
It starts off cloudy,
then it darkens.
The rain comes, and it pours,
and there's lightning, of course,
up above the thunder claps,
so loud and proud
letting all know it's here
like a hundred drummers
drumming all around.
Waters rising,
floods are coming
and wind is howling.
Now it's gusting,
bending trees back and forth.
House gutters are overflowing.
It passes over thankfully.
A storm at sea is a place not to be.
Lighthouses flash away
as though they are in competition
with the lightning flashes,
leaving storm chasers doing just that:
following and chasing data readings.
Summer storms,
some needed, some not.
So wet, yet sticky and warm,
bringing much needed rain
for the ground.

Giving that horrible
wet vegetation smell,
always lingering after a storm.

99 HANDS

You can have healing hands,
or touchy-feely hands.
Workers or shirker's hands.
Surgeon's hands
that are skilful healing hands.
Clapping hands.
Why not try
holding hands.
It gives so much joy
to young and old the same
as it goes. Love shows.
Join hands, join hearts,
lovers and best friends
through life's ups and downs.
Hands to hold a book,
fingers to turn pages in that book.
An artist's delicate flowing hands,
a potter's clay-shaping hands.
Tiny hands, so small, so cute.
Tiny hands leaving hand prints and fingerprints
behind
on furniture and walls.
At the time not funny,
but given time become
a happy memory.
Hands comfort us.

100 SOUP

Eating soup with a spoon
or drinking soup from a cup.
Slurping,
making noises like a duck,
some dripping in your lap.
You've got to love soup,
chicken and tomato,
too many to list them all
but these two are my
favourite soups of them all.
Hot soup in the winter
when snow is all around
is the best I found.
Slowly sipping inside
whilst looking outside.
Or do it another way,
a liquid meal
which makes you feel good inside,
ready to go outside
after dunking bread
or croutons instead.
Try left over soup or
make your own
from whatever's in your home.
Don't forget cold soup
chilled in the fridge,
to be devoured
on a hot summers day.

ABOUT THE AUTHOR

Darren Barker's novels and poetry have been, up to now, dark, deep and deadly. With this new collection, Darren has emerged from the darkness and doesn't skulk around in the shadows nearly as much as he used to. It's rumoured he even smiles, once in a while.

Darren lives a normal-seeming life, with a loving wife and children, in a quiet corner of Suffolk, weaving his word-pictures and quietly observing what lives in the shadows, and now, finally, the daylight.

Darren Barker's novels are currently available from amazon.co.uk -

Watching Twenty-Four Seven

Deadly Sexual Trance

Death is Coming

For the Family

Mitchel

along with his three volumes of dark poems:

Wrong – Dark Poetry

Creep – More Dark Poetry

Obscure – Yet More Dark Poetry

26913180R00094

Printed in Poland
by Amazon Fulfillment
Poland Sp. z o.o., Wrocław